Spiritual Chocolate

Spiritual Chocolate

Sweet Delights
for
Friends & Special People

Dr. Glenn Mollette

GMA Publishing & Inspiration Press
Newburgh, Indiana

Acknowledgements

This is for my wonderful friends and very special people. This book is dedicated to you. You have come through for me. You have stood by me. You have loved me and cared for me and been there for me. I thank you and dedicate this book to you. May the love and sincere appreciation that I have for you and desire to be your steadfast friend be evident in these very pages.

Cover Interpretation

The sweetest chocolates in the world are good friends and special people!

Contents

I Give You My Heart

L ove the Lord your God with all your heart, soul, strength and mind and your neighbor as yourself.

What does God want?

Does God want our attention on Sunday morning for an hour? That would be nice if we could at least give God one hour of attention. How much attention do you give God during the week? Does he have a lot of your attention in the morning, the noon, the evening time? Are you really tuned into the things of God, the word of God, the promises of God, the presence of God? Could we then at least tune in for just a little while when we come to church? How do you feel when you are talking to someone and they are looking at you but their mind is on someone else? Husbands, let's say you are talking to your wife...but while you are talking she is definitely thinking about another man. She is thinking about how another man smiles at her, compliments her and treats her. And it is clear that your wife is distracted and sometimes even uninterested. And you are able to read her mind and it makes you feel bad. That's how we treat God a lot. We treat Him this way during the week. We even treat Him this way on our dates with God. We have a weekly Sunday morning date with God and we show up sometimes very uninterested. Okay God, here I am, make me interested in you. Look good to me, God. Entertain me, God, the way I like to be entertained. Turn me on, God. God has already done back flips for us. He owes us nothing more. He has made us, sustains us and enables us to have all that we have; and we act like we are doing God a favor by giving him our attention?

When you are with your favorite person. Whoever that person may be – is it difficult to give that person your attention? No. You listen to what he or she says. Every word makes an impression on you. You are encouraged, blessed, helped, affirmed or even saddened because you underscore everything this man or woman says. You pay attention.

If you want to insult someone you ignore that person. You ever play that game? I'm not speaking to my husband this week. I'm not talking to my wife this week. I'm pouting—so the kids and I—we aren't talking this week. I don't like a certain church member so I will give him/her the cold shoulder treatment. So you put on your best prune face and extend your icicles and freeze the other person out.

You've heard of cold churches? One country preacher told of this cold church where it was so cold you could ice skate up and down the aisle. We've never had that problem in my home church. Our church is normally the church of the extended hand. Or, our church is where the handshake is a little slower and the arm is a little longer and the smiles are the warmest. But that is how it should be.

There are some significant people that need some of your attention. Now you can't pay attention to everybody. But there are significant people that God has brought into your life and one of the best gifts you can give to them is attention. And that doesn't go on a lot. People who share the same house and sleep in the same beds so often live lives that are worlds a part.

God wants your attention. Where is your mind now?

What does God want?

Does God want our money?

All God wants is my money. Why? Do you think God needs your money? Do you think He is having financial problems? God doesn't need your money. He already has it. He just currently has you on an allowance. He is giving to you. Your income is money that God gives to you. He owns the world. He gives us health to work and the ability to earn income. Why would we hesitate to be generous toward God? Why would we if God has blessed us with an income go for weeks and months and never give anything back to God?

Husband and wives give to each other. The attitude is everything is ours and whatever you need is yours. Every home has commitments and responsibilities but the husband doesn't' go for days and weeks without sharing his resources with his wife nor does the wife because there is a relationship of love, commitment and trust. There is the constant gift of giving in the family. There is nothing withheld.

You ever get stingy toward your mate? Sometimes financial scenarios change and every home has to tighten up just to keep the house financially afloat. Budgets have to change and certain expenses may have to be considered. But still you have the attitude toward each other that whatever we do have is yours and there is generosity. You are always giving.

Have you quit giving? Have you stopped giving to your husband or wife? Why? Don't you love them anymore? What changed your love? Are you going to pick up a Valentine card for your wife or husband this week? Are you going to buy them a box of candy or take them out to eat? Are you going to do anything special for that person you love? Why not? Not interested? He or she doesn't do much for you anymore? What made that change? What might happen in your home if both of you mutually shared and mutually would give?

Have you stopped giving to God? Has it been forever since you gave anything to God? Why not if no is your answer? Not interested? God just doesn't do much for you anymore? Has God ever stopped giving to you? Have you had to carry all the weight of the relationship? Mean old God...He makes me do it all. Is that true? Or does God keep giving to you and giving to you and giving to you and making a way for you and the relationship has become really one-sided?

What does God want? Some of our attention and devotion pleases God.

What makes you emotional? What makes you passionate? What is there in life that flips your switch? Jumping out of an airplane? A guy told me a few weeks ago that skydiving was his adrenaline rush. He said he forgets about everything else when he's jumping out of that plane. I think I can understand that.

Maybe you are passionate about your job. You love it. You live for it. It's your life. Nothing better than having a job you love and nothing worse than having one you don't.

Maybe you are passionate about your children. Their ballgames, homework and seeing them achieve their ultimate potential in life.

Or it may be a hobby that you enjoy.

But what happens with these things that have our passion? They dominate our time and our thoughts.

Folks, when you love somebody what happens? You want to know that person more. Let's get to know each other more we say. So we want to walk more together, talk more, do more, be together more. Guess what? We have the energy to do those things. We are always trying to create an opportunity to be with each other. There is a driving passion to find that time to be with each other. Or has that changed? Home life changed? Suddenly, you have no energy to do anything fun with the one you supposedly love? Not all that great to be with your husband or wife? When there is nothing else to do, do you spend time together? Twenty years ago you couldn't wait to take her out to eat...spend an afternoon...the whole day together. You said, "I love you so much I want to spend my entire life with you." And now it's, "Hey next week at 8 o'clock on Friday night we're going to try to get together ...if nothing happens." This is due a lot to both spouses having jobs, kids activities and everything under the sun that we let interfere with the relationship.

Are you passionate about God? Do you want to know Him more? Study His word...walk with Him more...talk more, do more? Have you ever been passionate about God? I want to tell you God is passionate about you! We read Romeo and Juliet and think that it's a love story. You watch something on television and say, "That's a love story." Remember that old movie, *Love Story*?

Nothing tops the Bible. God was willing to hang naked on a cross, beaten to a bloody pulp for you. God is pictured as the Shepherd who cannot rest that 99 of the 100 sheep are home. No, he is overwhelmingly distraught that one of the sheep is missing. It bugs God when one of his kids is missing; and he doesn't give up trying to reach a missing kid. God is the father who never gives up looking for a missing child and when the child comes home there is embracing, singing, and dancing and partying. The best food and the best clothes and the finest jewelry are all brought out because God is so passionate about you.

Doesn't a loving passionate God deserve a little in return? How can you help but be passionate toward God? Passion comes from within.

What does God want?

He wants your heart.

Where is your heart today?

Who has your heart?

Did God use to have your heart?

He wants the big picture. He wants your heart. Jesus said it. "Love the Lord your God with all your heart," but He added for extra emphases – "soul, strength and mind." Jesus was saying, *let me be sure you understand what I mean by heart – I mean everything.*

We love Him with our strength. We have energy for God. We have time to walk with God and talk with God and spend time with God. We have this strength for God but there is this heart that we have for Him. Our strength is renewed.

We love Him with our mind. God has our attention. We think about our relationship with our Father. We pay attention to what He is trying to tell us. We follow His direction.

We love Him with our soul. Our relationship with God reaches down within us. It touches every fiber of our beings. We are passionate about Him.

Today...how's your heart? Got heart trouble? I'm not talking about that muscle that keeps you alive. I'm talking about that dimension of your life that gives you life. Your heart gives your marriage life. You have your heart in it. Your heart gives your career life. You have your heart in it.

Your heart gives your hobbies life because you put your heart into them.

Jesus knew that your heart would do the same in your relationship with the Father.

CHAPTER ONE
FOR REFLECTION AND MEDITATION

1. Who is someone that needs some of your undivided attention?

2. How many directions is your attention divided on an average day?

3. What is consuming your heart at this moment?

4. How different would your relationship with God be if God had supremacy in your heart?

I Give You Time

Joshua 10:6 – 25 we have a story when the people of God were in battle against the Amorites.

In verse 9 we learn Joshua and the people marched all night from Gilgal and Joshua over took the enemy by surprise. The Lord threw them into confusion before Israel, who defeated them in a great victory at Gibeon. Israel pursued them along the road going up to Beth Horon and cut them down all the way to Azekah and Makkedah. In verse twelve, we read the Lord gave the Amorites over to Israel. Joshua said to the Lord in the presence of Israel: "O sun, stand still over Gibeon, O moon, over the valley of Ajalon. So the sun stood still, and the moon stopped, till the nation avenged itself on its enemies. As it is written in the book of Jasher, the sun stopped in the middle of the sky and delayed going down about a full day. There has never been a day like it before or since, a day when the Lord listened to a man. Surely the Lord was fighting for Israel!"

There was a time apparently when God gave the Israelites all the sunlight they needed for as long as they needed to accomplish their goal of winning the battle against their enemy the Amorites. The Bible refers to this occasion as the day when the Sun stopped and delayed going down about a full day.

It was as if Time stopped. God seemed to freeze nature long enough for his people to carry out a certain act. We can spend the rest of the time considering the background and theology of all of this but wouldn't it be something if Time could stand still?

If time could stand still – what part of time would you like to stand still? Your childhood? Your youth? Your early marriage years...your retirement years...or maybe a wonderful vacation? You thought at the time, "It would be great if it just stayed that way forever."

The reality is that time does not stand still for any of us. Time is moving on.

James 4:14 "What is your life? You are a mist that appears for a little while and then vanishes."

We commonly say that Jesus spent about three plus years in active ministry. We feel he was about thirty before he began to teach, preach and perform miracles and set his face in the direction of Jerusalem where he would die on the cross.

We are unclear what he did during his first 30 years. We have a glimpse of his early childhood but we don't know that much about his early life. Jesus may have performed many miracles during his young adult years but we don't know for sure.

We have the impression that Jesus lived a quiet life and worked...worked on his education...maybe even took care of his mother. We don't read about his father in his later life and it is assumed his father passed away.

Jesus spent his time doing the "daily" things of life. This is not a bad way to spend time—and many of us have to do the daily things.

We All Have Daily Duties

How much of your time is spent doing the daily? In my case there are teenagers in the house...normally I have Karen to care for...dishes to wash ...vacuum cleaner to run...washing machine...dryer...clothes to pick up. That goes on all the time. How much of your time is spent cooking, cleaning, picking up, straightening up, putting away, and it goes on every day? How many hours a day...a week do you spend with cleaning, clothes, dishes, dirt, food, and on and on? Two hours a day? More? How many hours a week? Seven? Fourteen? It may be very much your full time job and I could see that if I wanted to, I could easily spend 40 hours a week preparing meals, cleaning up dishes, doing laundry, doing something for the house.

So much of life is spent doing the daily things of life. Now they may be fun for you...mundane for another. Or you may be like me you try not to think about it and do whatever you have to do to get by.

We All Have Other Events

Weekly Events – Church on Sunday, prayer meeting, Bible study. Or it may be a civic meeting, athletic event, or ballgame.

Occasional Outings – could be dinner out, a concert, a sports event, a seminar, a fun event of some kind. You get dressed up and you're asked, "What's the occasion?"

Year Occasions – Christmas comes once a year, birthdays come once a year. New Year's eve...etc. come once a year. They certainly seem to come quickly. Anniversaries.

How many times a day do you do something you really want to do? How many times a week? How many times a month or during the year? How much time do you spend doing what you want to do?

I heard someone recently say, "I don't have the time to do the things I want to do...let alone the things I don't want to do." How much of your time is spent doing what you don't want to do? Eight hours a day? Hate your job? Many today do.

Are you miserable at home? Things just not right with your husband or wife? Is there trouble with the kids that's driving you crazy?

Does it seem like you just never get a day to just coast?

Life is short. Time goes by every day. How are you using your time?

My life is pretty simple. It seems when my day is done if I get to write about two hours and spend 30 minutes or so exercising that I feel fulfilled. But if I accidentally sleep past

6:00 in the morning it messes me up. I like to begin with my devotional thoughts about 4:00 and write to about 6:00 before we start the process of getting ready for school. Sometime before the day is over I like to fit some exercise in. It doesn't have to be in the morning. But I like to do it before six if possible. Seven o'clock exercise for me means I'm not going to be sleepy before ten or eleven o'clock.

I'm not saying that's all it takes to make me happy...there's a big difference. We need a lot to make us happy.

We are use to television's, heat, nice beds, cars... etc. I'm not talking about what it takes to make us happy or what we are use to. I'm talking about our time.

Time gets away from us. My mother is now in heaven. My father won't be around forever. I won't be here forever. We are like a mist. We come and go. Life is short.

Before you die there are some things you should try to do with your time. Personal business, family obligations, a will, set something aside financially for your church.

Before you die there are some things you should allow yourself to do with your time.

Before you die there are some things you had better do with your time.

Become at peace with God, make peace with others...make peace with your self.

Time is a great gift. Your relationship with God is your greatest. Your health is your second greatest. Time to enjoy these two is next in line. The greatest gift you can give to a friend or special person in your life is time.

Time to pray with them. For over eight years I've met almost every week with two or three men on Thursday morning at seven o'clock to pray. In that segment alone I've given these men at least 400 hours of my life. That's the equivalent of spending about 2 and ½ weeks nonstop with them. That's a lot of time that I spend with these guys. And I've spent enough time with them that I don't care what I say in front of them. But that's what happens when you spend time with people. You get to know them a little.

I have many acquaintances that I have not spend 30 minutes with my entire life and that's not bad...it's just that we haven't. People are busy. I stay busy. So sometimes it just doesn't happen.

Your time and my time is an incredible gift. Because when you give somebody time you are stopping everything else you could be doing to be with that person.

This is why marriages make it or suffer. There is little Quality time or no time. Kids and parents thrive or suffer because of well-spent quality time or no time together. Whatever person or project is going on, life makes it or suffers hinging on the time we give.

I give time to preparing sermons. I seldom go to a pulpit or lectern unprepared. I have, but only rarely.

When you give somebody time you are saying I care. I love you. I want to share in your life. I want to help you. You are important to me. I need you in my life. When we don't have the time of day for something or someone then we are saying just the opposite. We are saying, you are not important to me and I don't want to really be bothered by you. Now if you want time with me this week...and I can't fit you in, it doesn't mean you aren't important...it just means we will do it next week. If something is good...it's worth waiting on.

Jesus gave us time. He gave us his life. He gave us His ministry. He gave us Himself. He said in every human way...I love you. You are important to me.

And there is not a day that goes by that He doesn't want to spend time with you. He wants to meet you in prayer. He wants to meet you in His word. He wants to meet you in church.

This day and this week how will you spend your time?

What will you commit to accomplishing with some of your time this week or over the next month? Begin a life change? Begin something that you have been putting off? What will you do with your time?

Time is a Great Gift

Value your time – Your life and time are valuable.

Give your time – When any of us gives someone time we are expending valuable hours of life with one another.

Utilize your time – Make the most of life. Make the most of every moment. Make this moment count right now.

CHAPTER TWO
FOR REFLECTION AND MEDITATION

1. How do you enjoy spending your time?

2. What do you dread most doing?

3. Time is an incredible gift.

4. If you should live five more years...how will you utilize your time?

5. Do you have any time for God?

6. What is the best time you spend each week?

I Give You Friendship

I went out to find a friend and none were anywhere. I went out to be a friend and friends were everywhere.

A friend is someone who comes in when the rest of the world has walked out. You don't really know who your friends are until you have failed or messed up.

If you are successful you will have many superficial friends. If you failed or messed up you will have few superficial friends. The friends that you have will likely be real.

When you go up the ladder there are those who try to grab on and go with you. But when you fall down the ladder most people let you fall alone.

People normally need you when you are on top. They want to make appointments to see you. They want you to be a part of their organization. They want you in leadership. They want you on their membership list. They want to use your name when and wherever they might. But if you are on the bottom you are seldom invited to be a part of the "big dog" society or your name is not needed as a reference.

If you are doing good, people like to be seen with you. They want to sit with you at your table or they send special invitations to include you at their table. But if things are not necessarily well with you then people in general may not feel so inclined to be seen in your company.

Our perceptions of people always change after we have spent time with them. We know them better. We either like them more or like them less. We see them as being genuine or phony. We are attracted more to them or attracted less.

How many friends do you have?

How many people do you know? Not everybody that knows you is your friend. Some people may know you and not like you. And the more they know you...the more they dislike you. Some people know you and like you more. They see you for who you are and accept and appreciate you as a person.

One of the things I was finally able to do as a pastor several years ago was to begin to accept people where they are and not where I thought they should be. Few if any people in life are where we think they should be. People are not where we want them to be. They don't live for us. We are not where most people think we should be.

If We Would Be a Friend or Have a Friend, There Must Be:

Communication – Friendship begins and continues through communication. We talk and we talk a lot.

Acquaintances see one another. Acquaintances shake hands and say hello and exchange pleasantries. Friends talk. I have friends that I haven't talked to in a year or more. We are still friends...because we use to talk a lot. Our friendship is intact and when we talk we just pick up where we left off.

Honest Communication – Friendship has open and honest communication. Our conversations are very surface. "It's raining today. I wonder when the sun will shine. How are the kids doing? How's work going?" And we reply, "Yes it's raining today. The sun will shine tomorrow. Work is great...etc."

Sometimes we fear honest communication because we don't want to be a load to someone. We know that if we tell too much we may run people away. By and large people don't want to hear our gripes and complaints or about our struggles. We fear running off an acquaintance by talking too much. We don't want to unload on them.

There are probably only two or three or four people in your life that you can have serious honest communication. Probably that's all you need. It takes too much energy out of you trying to honestly and openly communicate with more than four or five people—especially if you ever ask for advice. You don't need advice from a dozen people because it will all likely be different and you'll just be more divided on what to do.

Who are you open with in your life? Who do you talk to and say, "I'm feeling great. I've had a marvelous day." Not everybody can stand that. It bugs some people if you're too happy. Who shares in your victories...rejoices with you in your accomplishments? Do you have anybody you can be honest with and say, "Hey, I made a million dollars this year." They in return will say, "Wow...that's great. I'm happy for you." Instead of most people who will say..."Wow...that's re..re..great...I'm hap ..hap..happy for you."

What about when you've blundered. Failed a class. Messed up a sale at work. Failed a project. Sinned against God. Who can you be honest with and say, "Hey, I messed up at work so bad today." And, whoever you are telling will genuinely listen and not only care, but will offer some comfort and sincere advice. Or, you are able to say to your friend, "I've sinned against God." And they listen and say, "I'm sorry that you've sinned. But, the Bible says, "If we confess our sins He is faithful and just to forgive us and cleanse us from all unrighteousness." Do you have anybody like that in your life that you can tell your sins to...and he/she will not condemn you? They will still love you and be your friend?

Long Distance Travel – How many people in life have you walked a long road with? Enoch was a man who walked with God and one day...God took him. I think that after many years of walking with God that one day God said, "Enoch you are closer to my place than yours...why don't you just come on home to be with me." And then, God took him on home. But Enoch walked with God for years.

I've walked with Karen for 26 years. Sometimes...I get so tired. I know she does and has said, "Glenn, I'm so tired of it." But the most emotionally fulfilling aspect of my life is caring for my wife. The most emotionally fulfilling thing I have done in the last month was driving to Dayton, Ohio…dressing my wife in her hospital bed…carrying her to my car, buckling her in…and sitting in the parking lot of McDonalds while I held a cup of water for her to sip through a straw.

Friendship is long distance travel. I had some friends in high school that I haven't seen since graduation. I roomed with a guy from high school at Georgetown and we thought we were friends but then we found out living together is different than just running around together and I haven't seen him in over 20 years. Never hear from him…and truthfully that makes me sad because we spent a lot of time together.

How many long distance people do you have in your life? Not many? Parents…children…a spouse…a hand full of people? People that just stick with you through sunshine, sleet, hail and the fog of life? Sometimes in the fog of life we lose people. It gets hard to see them…or we lose them. The hailstorms of life beat us down and beat up on our friends and they say…"We are too beat up by our friendship." They then walk away.

Do you have anybody in your life that has stayed with you through the fog and the hailstorms of life? Then, you have a friend.

Tolerance in Diversity – How many people in your life do you have a lot in common? Christianity brings people together. We may have that in common. But we have so much diversity.

We say, "We have Christ in common." But then we fall out over everything else. We are diverse in our interests.

Some like to talk about sports...some people hate sports. Some people love rock-n-roll music and some think it's awful. Some people like classical and some think classical is boring. Some like country music and some do not.

We get tangled up in our differences and therefore we have difficulty making friends with those that are different. We are all a little different.

A friend is someone that you can be comfortable around regardless of the diversity. That is tough because we are uncomfortable with people who are different or who like different things. So we seek out that which is common...our love for God, our adoption into God's family. He has adopted us and made us His children. Therefore we have the greater good in common.

1 Samuel 18:1 – 4 "After David had finished talking with Saul, Jonathan became one in spirit with David, and he loved him as himself. From that day Saul kept David with him and did not let him return to his father's house. And Jonathan made a covenant with David because he loved him as himself. Jonathan took off the robe he was wearing and gave it to David, along with his tunic and even his sword, his bow and his belt."

In 1 Samuel 20 we read about a chilling time. David's life is under threat by Jonathan's father, King Saul. "What is my crime" How have I wronged your father, that he is trying to take my life?" In verse 4, "Jonathan said to David, "Whatever you want me to do, I'll do for you."

Saul is definitely out to kill David...Jonathan now knows this and in verse 41 we have this touching scene of these two meeting…they kiss each other…they weep, but David, the Bible says, wept the most.

Vs. 42, "Jonathan said to David, "Go in peace, for we have sworn friendship with each other in the name of the Lord, saying, The Lord is witness between you and me, and between your descendents and my descendants forever.

A Willingness to Face Difficulty – Jonathan was a friend to David under the most difficult circumstances. His father hated David…and Jonathan loved him. Do you know anything about that? Are you a friend to anybody in just the worst circumstances? Like David and Jonathan there is stress and tears…and grief?

I think that's common. Friendship takes us through the best of times and through the worst of times. We laugh together and we cry together…because we are friends.

Proverbs 18:24 "A man that has friends must show himself friendly: and there is a friend that sticks closer than a brother."

That friend is our Lord Jesus.

John 15:15, "Love each other as I have loved you. Greater love has no one than this, that he lay down his life for his friends. I no longer call you servants, because a servant does not know his master's business. Instead, I have called you friends, for everything that I have learned from my Father I have made known to you.

You can tell Jesus anything and you might as well be honest. He already knows the truth. Whatever you tell him…he will still love you just the same. There is nothing you can tell Jesus that will shock him.

An old song says, "Are you burdened...are you heavy laden? Tell it to Jesus. You have no other such a friend or brother. Tell it to Jesus alone."

Jesus is in for the long haul. When you make Jesus your personal savior it is not a short-term adventure. He comes in to not stay awhile. He comes in to stay. Jesus said in John 10:27, "My sheep listen to my voice; I know them, and they follow me. I give them eternal life, and they shall never perish; no one can snatch them out of my hand." Do you need any long-term friends? Christ has promised us friendship for the long-term.

Jesus takes us where we are in life. He takes you just as you are. We sing this song all the time, *Just As I Am.* That means you come to God...sin and all. You don't have to achieve moral perfection to become a Christian because that never happens in this world. We spend all of life struggling in many ways. Yet, God says you come in all of your sins. I will forgive you and we will begin our long journey with where you are. We don't finish the journey and become a Christian. The journey begins when we become Christians.

Jesus never leaves us in times of difficulty. Hebrews 13:5, "God has said, never will I leave you; never will I forsake you. So we say with confidence, the Lord is my helper. I will not be afraid. What can man do to me?"

Today make this commitment. I will follow Jesus. There is no greater friend.

I will be a friend to somebody and I will begin today. I will trust God to lead me and take care of me as I do all that I honestly know that I can do to be a real friend.

CHAPTER THREE
FOR REFLECTION AND MEDITATION

1.   Do you have a friend?

2.   Who is your best friend and why?

3.   Friendship requires honesty and work.

4.   Have you tried being a friend to someone?

5.   How has God shown Himself friendly to you?

6.   Besides God, who is the one friend you can call upon about anything?

CHAPTER FOUR

I Give You Commitment

When was the last time you made a commitment? This week? Did you fill out some of the papers you received in the mail that will qualify you for a $25,000 credit card? You may have signed a document that says you will have the freedom to borrow money and pay it back with 21% interest tagged to it. Or, maybe you recently bought a car or a house and agreed to a monthly payment plan for a long time.

We make commitments like those all the time. We are committed to the utility companies and cable company and telephone people that we will use their services for a monthly cost. Those commitments are not the kind that we necessarily enjoy getting into – but we enter into them because we like running water, gas, electricity, television and all the other conveniences that our commitments bring to us. We receive the conveniences because of the commitment.

But what happens if we fail to meet the commitment? The water is turned off...the cable guy unhooks the television and the bank forecloses. Things are great as long as we honor our commitment. Life is not so good when we fail in our commitments.

Unforeseen Events Interfere with Commitments

Employment may change. The factory or business may shut down. There is a huge layoff and you are affected. Times change and the need for your work is altered. When unforeseen unemployment occurs it will likely affect our commitments.

Health may change. You may not always have good health. You may have decent health but it may get worse. You may have the ability to drive a car today but you may not tomorrow. You may be able to dig ditches today but you may not be able to tomorrow. You may have great energy today and abilities to wear a lot of hats and stamina to do all that is necessary, but tomorrow it may all change. As long as you are healthy you are able to maintain your commitments, but what if your health changes? It could likely make your ability to continue your commitment more difficult.

Life may change. Something may happen in the lives of your children. Your spouse may go through difficulties. Events may occur beyond your control. Now these events may underscore your commitment. They may make you stronger. They may break you. Our country rallied and is stronger because of events like 911. September 11 will always stand out as a day that changed our country and our world. That day has fortified millions in this nation. But how many people were forever broken by that terrorist attack? There are some who lost husbands or children or families and they have not gotten over that day. Life forever changed for them.

Howard Testerman is a life long friend of my father. He and my dad, my mother, and his wife, sang in a gospel quartet for years. They were really good. They had two daughters Norma and Leah Sue. I use to sit and watch television with Norma and Leah Sue for hours on Friday night while they would practice in another part of the house. Luella Mae, Howard's wife, Norma and Leah Sue were all beautiful, smart, talented women. One day we received a call that Luella Mae was hit in her Volkswagen head on by a drunk driver and was killed almost immediately it seemed. Her life being snuffed out was traumatic to the community. My mother and father tried singing with Howard after that but it was never the same and they soon quit. Life had changed.

A few years later Norma lost a handle on life and killed herself. She took a gun and ended it all. And then I received word that over the weekend Leah Sue who was doing great in her own construction business was burned in a fire. The house completely burned around her and all that they could find was the chimney and her bones lying in what was once her bed. Heartbreaking.

I asked my sister, "How is Howard doing?" "Not so great." I don't think he has given up on his faith. I'm sure his love for God is just as great as ever...but sometimes events happen to us that radically change life.

What are some of the biggest commitments that you have made in life? Possibly your commitment to Jesus is your biggest commitment of all. Your commitment brings you to church two or three times a week. Your commitment has you giving a large portion of your income to support God's work. So your time and money and a lot of your emotion and heart is tied up in the Lord's work.

Your commitment to your spouse and family may be your second biggest commitment. You love your family. You care for them. You provide for them. You are very involved in what they are doing. Your spouse and family is a 24-hour a day life.

Your job may be your third commitment. It may require eight, ten or more hours a day. You love your job, or you need your job or enjoy working and so therefore you are very committed to you work.

What commitments in life have you broken? Did you say you would do something and you didn't follow through? Did you say you would always stick with God and serve Him but lately you haven't been too committed?

Did you say you would always be faithful to your husband or wife but somewhere along the way you broke that commitment? Did you tell somebody you would pray for him or her but you haven't? Did you tell somebody you would always be friends but you really aren't friends any more? Did you tell somebody you would do a job but you haven't?

Have you ever broken a commitment? In some way we all have. To some degree we have all been unfaithful in different areas of life. We have good intentions. We mean well.

We mean what we say at the time but then life may change and we are hindered or life is altered for us in some way.

One of the greatest gifts you may offer someone is commitment. I'll be your husband or wife…forever. When it's at all possible I will be at my church. "Let us not give up meeting together as some are in the habit of doing, but let us encourage one another – and all the more as you see the day appearing," Hebrews 10:25. I will be at work every day. Or, I will also be committed to taking my days off.

Who or what do you have a commitment to in life? Is it your spouse, children, God, a friend, your career or your hobbies?

God is committed to us. Hebrews 13:5 "I will never leave you or forsake you." That is commitment.

Jesus sent his disciples out and said, "I am with you always. Even unto the end of this age."

Romans 8 says, "What shall we say to these things, "If God be for us who can be against us.

God is committed to us. His commitment does not waver. Aren't you glad you don't have to worry about the commitment of God? There is no shadow of turning with God. He is not one way today and another way tomorrow. He is the same yesterday, today and tomorrow," Hebrews 13:8.

Today, give thanks that God loves you and is committed to you. Who is someone that needs your commitment? Give it to them. Let them know that you are with them. Let them know you love them and you are standing with them in prayer. Do something tangible to let them know.

Commitment is only a word. It takes a life of love and expression to back it up.

God did more to demonstrate commitment than he did talking about it. Jesus was a demonstration of God's commitment to mankind. The word became flesh and dwelt among us. He left heaven to prove his commitment. He then hung naked on a cross and sinful people drove nails into his hands and feet. There on a cross he died for us. God was and is committed to us today. He loves you. As God has loved us let us extend love and commitment to others.

CHAPTER FOUR
FOR REFLECTION AND MEDITATION

1. How has God proven His commitment to us?

2. Your greatest commitment is to whom? Why?

3. Have you ever broken a commitment?

4. Has God ever broken a commitment to us?

5. Has anybody ever shown commitment to you?

6. What does commitment mean to you?

I Give You Confidence

John 21: 15 "When they had finished eating, Jesus said to Simon Peter, "Simon, son of John, do you truly love me more than these?" Yes, Lord, he said, "You know that I love you." Jesus said, "Feed my lambs." Again Jesus said, "Simon, son of John, do you truly love me? He answered, "Yes, Lord, you know that I love you." Jesus said, "Take care of my sheep," The third time he said to him, Simon, son of John, do you love me?" Peter was hurt because Jesus asked him the third time, "Do you love me?" he said, "Lord, you know all things; you know that I love you." Jesus said, "Feed my sheep."

We read the story of Peter in the book of John very understandably. He has recently denied the Lord and embarrassed himself by denying Jesus in his final hours. He feels lousy about himself. His head is down. His shoulders drooped. The bold charismatic man has become quiet because he has lost confidence.

Jesus is always the master teacher and Jesus sets about doing what only He could do and that is to restore the confidence of Peter.

"Peter do you love me? Yes Lord, you know I love you. Then feed my sheep replied Jesus." This discourse goes on three times. This is Jesus reaching out to an unconfident Peter. Amazingly Peter comes back. The sword wielding thundering stand up man for God who is reduced to a denying cowardly man is brought back by the only one who could and that was Jesus. Peter would later preach as boldly as any man could preach on the day of Pentecost. And we never read again about Peter showing any signs of lacking confidence again. He moved and preached and witnessed for Jesus like no other in the book of Acts.

It is incredible what Jesus can do for our confidence. Jesus restored Peter's confidence. When you and I sin, fall down, make mistakes or run off the road of life, it un-levels us. We lose our confidence because – we failed. Failure, sin and mistakes blatantly call to our attention that we are human beings who have a lot of room for error. We make errors in judgment. And when we do, they always show up and steel from us our confidence.

Jesus gives confidence! Why? Because He loves us and forgives us so much! Who is the person or the people who give you confidence? It's the person who loves you and is always forgiving you. He or she says to you that I love you. I don't care that you messed up. I really don't want you to do it again.

I believe in you. I have confidence in you. You are great. You can do it. When people love us even when we have failed and say, "I believe in you. I forgive you. I love you. Then we say, here is someone who cares about me. I need to arise to the occasion.

Peter truly arose to the occasion and became a man on fire for Jesus. Jesus gave him confidence in himself.

We need confidence. We need to give it to others. We need to extend confidence to people.

When you came to Christ and turned from sin and turned to him how did it make you feel? You felt better. You felt good. You felt relieved. You felt clean and you felt saved. And you knew you had not become all that you wanted to be but you also knew that suddenly you were not what you use to be. Your confidence level changed. You suddenly felt better about you. You felt better about your future. You felt better because the old suddenly had passed away and all things had become new. You felt new.

Do you feel that way? Do you feel confident in Christ? Old things have passed away. All things have become new. We are new creations in Christ.

Who gives us confidence? God gives it to us. Greater is He that is in us than he that is in the world. God gives us our confidence.

Therefore, we should extend confidence. That's not always easy. We are prone to tear into people. When people frustrate us or let us down we want to give them an ear full. We want to sound off. You see we carry these little frustrations around with us every day. We have to deal with daily life. We face traffic, house chores, finances and relationships that keep us stirred up. Then, when somebody that we are close to disappoints us then we feel we can freely tear into them and give them our pent up frustrations. What happens is we may destroy a relationship but we also may rip into the person's confidence. Our goal in life should never be to harm a brother or sister. Jesus could have been like a lot of people. He could have ripped into Peter and said, "Peter...you failed the church. Peter...you failed me. Peter...you let us all down." Jesus could have grinded his heel into the side of Peter. What did Jesus do? Hey Peter...get over it. Get on with life. It's okay. Feed my sheep.

If Peter had been a member of our church would we have said, hey Peter...we all make mistakes come back and teach Sunday school. Or, Peter...you're human, by the way you going to be here to preach for us Sunday? We hope so Peter. No...I'm afraid we would have said, Peter you blew it and we can't use you anymore. We will be watching you from now on Peter. Peter would have blown our confidence. But his mistake didn't foil Jesus' use for him one bit. Frankly, Peter's greatest service came after he had blown it. Fortunately Jesus gave him the chance.

Has somebody ever extended confidence to you after you blew it? Is there somebody you need to reach out to and extend confidence in them even though they have greatly failed? It might be the greatest gift that you might ever give to someone. A part of our Christian ministry is to reach out to people in love. What does that mean? It means restoring them to service. In the Christian faith we normally just shoot our wounded. You broke your leg? Bang...you're shot dead and done. Jesus restored Peter. He would have restored Judas too if Judas would have given him a chance. Judas lost all confidence in him self. Rightly so he blundered in such a horrible way. But Jesus was going to the cross for sinners just like Judas. Though our sins be as scarlet he makes them as white as snow.

A part of our ministry is to encourage people. But have you heard anything like the following: "I don't want to encourage him/her too much they might get the big head." How many people do you know that have the big head? How many people do you see walking around with confidence in them selves and confidence about life? Arrogance surely turns us all off. Humility with success is very attractive. But the average person does not want to teach a Sunday school class not because they can't...it's because they lack the confidence. They won't sing a solo in church because they don't have the confidence. They won't lead in prayer in church because they lack the confidence. They are afraid of failure.

Our job is to encourage people and say...I believe in you. I know you can...or you should. I see your talent or your potential. I think you are great. How many people need that from you?

I need it. I need it from my wife. I need to hear from her. Glenn, I really love you. I really thank you for what you do for me. You are a great husband. She in turn needs to hear the same from me. I need it from my children. I don't mind busting my skin for my kids, and when my 16 year old comes to my door and says goodnight dad I love you, that's about all I need to go another day. When I make mistakes and embarrass my friends...don't act like you don't know me. You pray for me and love me.

I was so irritated at Zach one morning. He missed his school bus. I really didn't have the 20 minutes to take him to school. And I sounded off as I normally do and said all the things that made me feel better. You've got to get out of bed. You need to do some of this stuff you are doing at night before you go to bed. You are staying up too late. Well...after I had released my frustration on him I knew I had to start doing damage repair. Plus I was right in the middle of writing this when he came back in the door and said, "I've missed the bus."
I got control of the tone of my voice. Told him I wanted him to have a good day...that I loved him and to be sure to bring his assignments home. It's so hard to know sometimes how much to reprimand a person. Sometimes we can wound them so bad that they are never again any use to anything or anybody. Honestly, I think we wound people sometimes and we really need to guard our speech.

A good word may save a soul. A bad word may lead to destruction. Now I told you I needed it. You do too. You need to hear it from your husband or wife - everyday. You need to hear it from family and from your friends. You need it from the church too and from me. We need to give that to each other. We get busy and we don't extend confidence.

I think Jesus was almost hunting Peter down after his resurrection to restore his confidence and his usefulness to the kingdom. Can you think of anybody like that? Anybody ever just hunt you down to say...I'm here for you. Whatever it is...regardless...we are friends and I am here for you. Anybody you need to look up...hunt down and say to them, "God loves you. I love you. I'd like to see you utilizing your life for God and for good things."

You could be the very person that encourages someone just enough to turn their life around. You may jumpstart them to go back to work. You might help restore their love for God, others or even you.

Jesus wanted Peter to love him. Peter...I want to know. I want to hear from your mouth...do you love me?" "Lord...you know I love you." "Well then Peter feed my sheep."

Later...in this same section of scripture Jesus would say to Peter... "Follow me."

CHAPTER FIVE
FOR REFLECTION AND MEDITATION

1. We all need encouragement and confidence in
    ourselves.

2. Discouragement can render us almost useless. What
    has discouraged you lately?

3. How did Jesus encourage people who had failed?

4. How did Peter fail and how do we sometimes fail like
    him?

5. Do you know anybody today that could use a word of
    encouragement?

6. How might you today help restore someone's
    confidence?

CHAPTER SIX

I Give You Forgiveness

Mathew 18: 23 – 35, "Therefore the kingdom of heaven is like a king who wanted to settle accounts with his servants. As he began the settlement, a man who owed him ten thousand talents was brought to him. Since he was not able to pay, the master ordered that he and his wife and his children and all that he had be sold to repay the debt. The servant fell on his knees before him, ' Be patient with me, he begged and I will pay back everything.' The servant's master took pity on him canceled the debt and let him go. But when that servant went out, he found one of his fellow servants who owed him a hundred denarii. He grabbed him and began to choke him. 'Pay back what you owe me,' he demanded. His fellow servant fell to his knees and begged him, 'Be patient with me, and I will pay you back.' But he refused, instead, he went off and had the man thrown into prison until he could pay the debt. When the other servants saw what had happened, they were greatly distressed and went and told their master everything that had happened. Then the master called the servant in, 'You wicked servant, he said, 'I cancelled all that debt of yours because you begged me to. Shouldn't you have had mercy on your fellow servant just as I had on you?' In anger his master turned him over to the jailers to be tortured until he should pay back all he owed. 'This is how my heavenly Father will treat each of you unless you forgive your brother from you heart."

This man received a lot of understanding and forgiveness – but he didn't extend understanding and forgiveness.

A sad reality of life is that we want forgiveness but are more reluctant to give forgiveness. The man in the story was forgiven for a huge debt and then almost immediately after his release sees somebody that owes him a few dollars and almost literally tries to wring it out of him.

Forgiveness is another chance. Sometimes it's many chances because we have been forgiven and forgiven and forgiven.

Forgiveness is a clean slate. Justified before God. Justified means we have a clean slate.

The reality of forgiveness is that we all need it. All of us make mistakes and mess up. We enjoy the forgiveness of God and hope we will receive it from our fellowman. In turn we need to grant forgiveness.

Mates have to forgive mates. No marriage relationship can survive without forgiveness. Partners should work hard to never fail a companion. But, we err. Error can create lifelong bitterness if not dealt with and forgiven. When someone makes a mistake it's always nice to hear, "I failed. I'm sorry. I repent. I'll try by God's grace to not make that error again." A heart that recognizes that he or she erred goes a long way in helping someone to be forgiving toward him. Arrogance in failure is more difficult. If someone does not want to be forgiven and shows no signs of remorse or repentance then it is more difficult to feel forgiving toward that person – just a fact of life. There is a limit to this though. The person who feels sinned against should not hold a persons nose to the grind that has failed. Error is not a justified excuse to hurt somebody – although emotionally you may feel very revengeful. Forgiveness may have to sit down and think, pray and have sometime along. Forgiveness may need some hours of conversation with the person about the failure. Hopefully some kind of understanding can be achieved. A commitment from both sides to work to prevent it from happening again should be agreed upon. After this …life needs to find a way to go on.

If you don't find a way to give forgiveness then you will have few friends and relationships in life – likely none. Any relationship/friendship will come to the crossroads of forgiveness. One in the party will need it and the other will be have to decide if it is to be granted. If it is withheld…the relationship by all means is crippled…and maybe even terminated because a relationship/friendship can't survive without forgiveness. Bitterness sets in and distrust will prevail and it becomes a very unhealthy environment for any future relationship/friendship growth.

Give your friend or special person forgiveness. It may take some time and hard work. It may require heart -wrenching conversation and prayer but in the end you may still have a friendship and relationship that will experience growth and even flourish enriched by the soil of love, understanding and forgiveness.

CHAPTER SIX
FOR REFLECTION AND MEDITATION

1. Are you forgiven of your sins?

2. Have you accepted God's love and forgiveness?

3. Is there someone today that you need to forgive?

4. As you accept forgiveness from God are you willing to give it to others?

5. We all sin and fail in life. No one is perfect. Where is forgiveness most needed in your life today?

CHAPTER SEVEN

I Give You Help

Hebrews 13:5 and 6, "For He hath said, I will never leave you, nor forsake you. So that we may boldly say, "The Lord is my helper."

Genesis 2:20, "but for Adam no suitable helper was found. So the Lord God caused the man to fall into a deep sleep, and while he was sleeping, he took one of the man's ribs and closed up the place with flesh. Then the Lord God made a woman from the rib he had taken out of the man, and he brought her to the man."

Exodus 4:7, we have the story of Moses and his reservation about being the one to lead God's people. God said, "You shall speak to him and put words in his mouth; I will help both of you speak and will teach you what to do."

Mark 2: 1 - 5 "A few days later, when Jesus again entered Capernaum, the people heard that he had come home. So many gathered that there was no room left, not even outside the door, and he preached the word to them. Some men came, bringing to him a paralytic, carried by four of them. Since they could not get him to Jesus because of the crowd, they made an opening in the roof above Jesus and, after digging through it, lowered the mat the paralyzed man was lying on. When Jesus saw their faith, he said to the paralytic, son, your sins are forgiven."

Philippians 4:13, "I can do all things through Christ."

We Need Help

When we are babies we need help. In Bethlehem little innocent babies lost their lives. They were defenseless to an arrogant king. Babies need the very most basic care. They have to be nourished and cared for in every way. Babies have to be helped with everything.

When they are sick somebody has to take them to the doctor. A baby can't drive himself to the doctor. A baby can't get up and walk to the bathroom or bath him self. A baby can't turn on the light or turn it off.

When we are youngsters we need help. We are taught how to tie our shoes. But somebody has to teach us. We are taught how to shower and brush our teeth...but somebody starts us out. We are taught how to run a lawn mower, wash dishes, say our ABCs, read and write.

When we are young adults we need help. Kids in college need a lot of help. Mostly they need money...but guidance and much prayer. Young adult married couples starting out can always use help sometimes with housing, cars, furniture...you name it. And when young adults start having babies then they need help in caring for those grandchildren.

When we are adults we need help. Sometimes we may need a reference for a job or someone to help us in finding a job. Sometimes we may need someone to talk to or just listen.

When we are seniors we need help. I see a lot of productive 80 year-old people. But...the body is not as able ...unless you are Caleb. This astonishing Old Testament character was 85 and a mountain climber.

When we are sick we need help. Four men carried a sick man to Jesus. What would have happened to this man if he had not been helped? He likely would have just been cast to the side of the road begging for help.

We need help when we are dying. I wanted so badly to help my mother on September 3, 2001. I couldn't help her. But the nurses and doctors in the hospital helped her by keeping her comfortable as much as possible.

Years ago some of us stood around a great preacher's room and we held hands and prayed as he went out into eternity. Just earlier he had asked me to read Hebrews chapter 11 to him.

When we are hurting we need help. A woman in the Bible said, if I can but touch the hem of his garment I will be healed. And she was healed. But what do you do when you are hurting? This woman sought out Jesus and he helped her. If you will keep your eyes on Jesus he will help you when you are hurting.

When we have failed we need help. Peter had failed the Lord. He just plain and simple failed. And Jesus in John's gospel three times restored Peter by asking him to feed his sheep.

We can't save ourselves—we need help. God helped us by giving his son Jesus to die on the cross. We would be miserably lost without all that God did for us in Christ.

We don't know the way to heaven…we don't know for sure of the location of heaven…which way is really up out there? We are desperate for the help of God to get to heaven after we die.

He Will Help Us

We can't create oxygen to breath; we can't create sunshine, or make more dirt. We can't save life from dying. We can't make life perfect for people. We can help people. But we can't make life great for them.

There is a limit to help. Sometimes you just run out of fuel. We give up. We try. But then we get exhausted.

God is unlimited. I'm not saying we can backhand God every morning and night and say here, "take this." But God gives us a lot of rope. 2 Peter 3:9, He is long suffering toward us. He keeps helping us.

He helps us when we don't deserve it. Romans 5:8, God commends his love toward us.

He helps us when we ask him to. "Ask and it shall be given."

He helps us in spite of ourselves. He is a loving Father that is making a way for us even when we are unaware. One of the best things you can do for a friend or special person in your life is throw them a lifeline and help them. I know we exhaust our resources. We become exhausted mentally, physically and financially. We get to the point where we say, "No more. I can't." And that happens often.

But God never runs out of resources. If we do not turn our face from him God has an unlimited supply of help. The Bible says He is our helper.

Who is someone today…that needs your help?

Is it you? Do you need some help?

Do you need God's help?

CHAPTER SEVEN
FOR REFLECTION AND MEDITATION

1. Have you ever needed help?

2. Give thanks for someone who one time came to your rescue.

3. Is there anybody you might help today or this week?

4. How has God helped in your life?

I Give You Honesty

What do you owe people? Not a whole lot...maybe courtesy...but that doesn't abound in society today. It's nice when we see it or receive it. An honest days work. If you are an employee it's only fair. Abide by the laws of our country. Pay your taxes and try not to break the law. Be right toward persons. Do unto others as you would have them do unto you.

But what do you owe people? Is it anybody's business what your income is? Let's say for instance you make $8 an hour...or if you make $80 an hour...unless you want to tell that, the only person that has to know...is the IRS.

If you go to the doctor for an examination on your left hand index finger, is that something that everybody is supposed to know? No...it's nobody's business unless you decide to tell somebody.

You have people that ask you stuff like ...how much did your car cost? How much are your house payments? How

much do you weigh? How old are you...all these
questions...and truthfully your information about you as a
person is your personal information unless you really want to
tell it.

Did you ever think about this...read carefully...if you
want somebody to know something about you, what will you
do? You will make a big deal to tell them...right? Or, if there is
something that somebody wants you to know about, they are
going to make a big deal to let you know.

If they don't tell you, then maybe they didn't feel it was
vital information. Maybe they just figured it was none of your
business or maybe they were unsure what to really say.

Now I think I'm blatantly honest. If you don't think so buy
Silent Struggler...or *Nursing Home Nightmares*. I've chronicled
things about my personal life that most people would never do.

Somebody asked me the other day "Pastor, are you
and your wife able to have sex? I almost pulled a Simon Peter. I
almost withdrew my sword and I would have not gone for his
ear. What amazed me, was this guy thought—I guess—that it
was okay to ask that question. Now I wrote very candidly about
our sex life in *Silent Struggler*...in chapter 12. The book can be
ordered via any bookstore or via the Internet. But if I want you
to know anything more personal about that I'll come to you
and tell you.

Let's say, I come to you and ask, "How much money
do you make?" Wouldn't that be kind of a personal question?
What if I asked you, "How much money do you have in the
bank?" Would that not be kind of personal? What if I asked you

about you and your spouse's intimate life wouldn't you think...you're getting kind personal aren't you?

There is a lot about ourselves that we are entitled to keep private, although, I've hung a lot of my life out for others to read about. But that was a decision that I made after much prayer and struggle.

Now if someone volunteers information that's another matter. And some people do. They volunteer everything they know. They will tell you about everything they are doing and where they are going, what time they are going to be there, and when they are going to leave. They will tell you what time they started and what time they finished and all that happened in between as though everybody cares. I go visit people from time to time and sadly the only way they feel they can get any attention is by griping. So they complain about this ache and this pain. And they go into long discourses about all their troubles. And I want to ask, is there anything good going on in your life?

Or, you know people that start out "I was on the west side of town at 7 a.m. and then I was eating breakfast at 8:00 and then I was in a meeting at 8.30 and then I was driving in my car at 9, now I will be on the north side of town at 11:00 and in Henderson at noon. I know some preachers like that they'll tell their whole calendar for the week like the whole world revolves around what they are doing. When truthfully, few people really care.

By and large there is not a lot of information we owe generally everybody. But real close-knit relationships involve a lot of honesty, and you can't have that with everybody. You can have it with your spouse. One or two friends, children, and that's about it.

I asked a lady what is the one gift you want from someone special in your life and she said, "Honesty...the truth."

You want the truth from your husband. Where you been? You see, you can ask that of a spouse and expect to get an honest answer.

Do you love me? Do I make you happy? Is there something wrong?

You can ask that of your children and children can ask questions of parents and there should be honesty. You may have a couple of dose friends that you are blatantly transparent with.

On the same token this doesn't mean we lie to others who are not family or close friends. You either tell the truth, or you just say I don't want to talk about that.

In the New Testament, Peter was asked a question and he lied about it. I don't know him. I don't know Jesus.

In the Old Testament, Jacob lied to his daddy and said he was Esau. The serpent lied to Eve about the fruit of the tree. Ananais and Sapphira lied to the church. They said they had sold a plot of ground and we are going to give the money to the church. They didn't have to give the money to the church. It was theirs. They could have done what they wanted. But they lied about it.

Jesus said, "And you shall know the truth and the truth shall set you free." The truth is like a sword—its sharp, sometimes painful, but healing. The surgeon's knife performs the task, but set's the stage for correction and then healing.

The truth is like correction that set's the stage for healing. The truth sets us free. If you cannot tell the truth you will always live in bondage. When we lie we are binding ourselves. When we are honest we set ourselves free.

The devil is the Father of lies. And the devil binds us. He bound Adam and Eve. He tripped them up with God. He's good at that ...he binds us...enslaves us to a lie.

The Bible has many examples. Ananais and Sapphira lied to the church. They didn't have to. They lied about their giving and their sacrifice. They didn't have to. If you don't financially support the church you don't have to act like you do. I don't think you should be in a place of leadership if you have an income and don't give. If you make money and don't give anything you shouldn't be in a place of leadership. Be honest.

We are dishonest when we don't have to be— Annanais and Sapphira. We are dishonest under pressure— Peter, "I don't know him." Not a flattering moment in the life of Peter.

Has anybody ever lied about you?

Has anybody ever lied to you?

Has anybody ever lied for you?

The devil is the father of lies. He was a liar from the beginning. He lied to Adam and Eve. He lies about everything.

Isaiah 14: 12 – 14 record the origin of Lucifer or Satan's fall from heaven. "I will raise my throne above the stars of God...I will make myself like he most high." After his dismissal from heaven we see his place of deceit at work – planet earth. In the very beginning of man's peaceful existence he sets about his destructive way of undermining God's creation until he brings about the fall of man.

A friend is someone who can handle the truth and still be a friend. Someone who loves you wants to know the truth so they can help you.

Now an enemy may seek to use the truth against you. But a friend needs to know the truth so he or she may be a better ally. An enemy takes the truth and runs with it. They are like the town crier.

The truth binds us with people. When they know us and can know the truth about us and still love us and be a friend then we have someone special.

Often our relationships hinge on prerequisites. There are stipulations. And because of the stipulations we feel forced to maintain those even when we have swayed from what may be expected.

Ananais and Sapphira probably felt under pressure to do what everybody else in the church were doing and therefore lied so they would fit in with everybody else.

Peter was dishonest under pressure. And then we see Peter's regret and his embarrassment. "Satan has desired to sift you." The Devil is after you Peter.

His denial was a lie. I don't know Jesus. Sure you do Peter. You are the one, who said, "You are the Christ." You stood with Jesus on the Mt. of Transfiguration and watched Jesus bring Lazarus back to life. You know Jesus real well. I think that is why Peter's denial—his dishonesty—was so painful. Because hours earlier he was flaying his sword to protect Jesus and now he is vehemently lying that he even knows him.

And then when it is over he feels so useless that he can hardly raise his head. Jesus would come back to life and resurrect from the grave. And one of his first tasks would be to restore Peter who had messed up.

Peter would be the bold man of God in Acts and would be used in a mighty way.

A rich gift for your friends and special people—is the truth. Give them honesty.

I give you my truth about who I am.

About how I feel

About what I believe

About what I can do

About what I can't do

And, about what I would like to do - my intentions.

Now in most cases it may be immaterial, because you don't have that many friendships and relationships with which you need to release so much of yourself. There is a lot that is just nobody's business...unless you want to make it their business.

When I wrote *Silent Struggler* I wrestled with honesty. I thought how could I write a care-giving book unless I'm honest. I can't help anybody if I'm not.

We lie because we don't want to disappoint people. We want to convey a certain image. Seems like once upon a time I watched a TV game show called, *To Tell The Truth*. And there were three persons who would all testify to being the same person. They would give what seemed credible testimony. There would be a panel of 4 or 5 people who would ask questions trying to determine who was telling the truth. Sometimes the contestants would be so good that the panel could not discern who was or was not being honest. And not everybody would guess whom the person was that was really telling the truth. When the game was over the TV host would ask, "Would the real Mr. John Doe please stand?" Some in the audience would be amazed as to who the real Mr. Doe really was.

Today, will the real you, please stand up. Who are you? What is your name? What kind of a person are you? What do you enjoy doing? Where do you like to go? What do you enjoy for entertainment? Of what does your daily life consist? So often our lives are like the game show... *To Tell The Truth*.

Do we ever lie? How do you feel? Feel great. How do you think I look? You look great. How is life? Marvelous. Do we ever lie to others? Do we ever lie to God? Do we ever lie to ourselves?

Lies We Often Tell

I'm going to start.

I'm going to quit.

I'm going make things right.

I'm going to try.

Fabrication – we make something up.

Exaggeration – we fudge a little on the truth.

What happens when you tell the truth? You're free.

Now, some people don't like the truth. You may even have to pay some penalty for the truth.

Adam told the truth and didn't have to hide anymore. Jesus came and was truth. He said, "I am truth." He embodied truth.

Sometimes the truth is painful and so is surgery. But when the surgery is over it gives way to healing. The truth gives way to a full relationship or friendship. Here are two people, but there is mass dishonesty between the two. The dishonesty is like a barrier. And the more the dishonesty, the more the blockade becomes. If there are lies, resolve them. If there has been dishonesty set the record straight.

The truth releases the power within you. Any kind of lying suppresses your power. Tell a lie, it suppresses you. It holds you down. But when you tell the truth you are able to burst forth. You come out. Why? The truth is powerful.

The devil is the father of lies. When Peter lied he went into hiding. It suppressed him. Paul couldn't lie about Jesus. His honesty and passion for Christ landed him in jail...caused him to get beat up...ended up costing him his life. But his honesty and internal truth freed him to stand before men and kings and declare Jesus is the Son of God. Therefore he traveled and preached Jesus. He lived and talked about Jesus and wrote writings read by more people than anybody else. Jesus set him free.

So the truth releases your potential. The truth releases your power. The truth releases your person.

Dishonesty inhibits you. Dishonesty keeps you from ever realizing your real goals and dreams. You'll never achieve your ultimate potential if you don't learn to stand for the truth.

Real truth is seen on the cross. And that truth is that we are sinners. Sin put Jesus on the cross. Your sins and mine put Jesus on the cross. You are a sinner. The Bible says we all are and Jesus had to die on the cross for your sins.

The truth is that sin is ugly and awful. You want to see how pretty your little white sins are look at the cross and see Jesus. He was beyond recognition of a man.

The truth is that if you die in your sins you will go to hell when you die. Jesus talked about hell more than heaven. He said man is lost and He came seeking to save the lost. If you totally ignore what Jesus did for you on the cross, the Bible says you will die lost.

What do you need to be honest about? Are you a Christian or not? Do you love Jesus or do you just attend church? Will you go to heaven when you die? Why? Are you honest about your life? This is my life.

Did you ever steal $5? What about $10, a $1,000? How long are you going to keep that hidden? Is it really worth it? If somebody asks you, did you take that $10 and you say yes, then arrangements can be made to clear the matter. You may be given the opportunity to pay it back. You might be forgiven and nothing said. There is an opportunity to deal with it. You can deal with the known. You can deal with the truth. But you can't deal with the unknown.

When you steal $10 or whatever from someone, then the other party is left wondering what happened to it? Who took it? How did it disappear? Why did it disappear? How did this happen? And then finally it comes out that you took it...and so now not only have you stolen but you are a liar and very untrustworthy.

If you are a thief, just say, "I'm a thief." There is help for you. Now, it's embarrassing. The devil is a thief. Judas was a thief. He stole from Jesus. Anybody that will steal from Jesus will steal from anybody. Did you ever steal anything from Jesus? Don't be a thief, don't steal, the Bible says don't do it.

Achan took some spoils from war that he was not supposed to take and it caused he and all the Israelites trouble. Do you embezzle money from work? Do you steal from your family? Do you take money from others and do something else with it you are not supposed to? It will cause you trouble and everyone else.

The thief breaks in and steals. It is taking something that doesn't belong to you. Get a job, friend, you don't have to steal.

I am amazed at how many people will give you the shirt off their backs. If there is anybody who has a real need in our community I know our church will try to meet the need. We don't turn people away who really need food or clothes. If somebody in our church needed something, we would try to help.

Do you ever lie? Ananaias said that they were giving all their money from the sale of some property to the church. They didn't have to but they lied about it. And they dropped over dead. They were carried out. They lied when they didn't have to. You don't have to lie about anything. Are you a drug addict? We will pray for you. Are you an alcoholic? Are you a sex addict? Have you got a problem with stealing? Don't keep it up. Some things are hard to admit, but friend, just tell the truth. It will set you free. We may not make you the church treasurer. We wouldn't want to give you that temptation. We might not want to put you in charge of handing out gospel tracts at the local liquor store if you are an alcoholic…that might not be a good idea. But there is some other place that you can serve and we can help you.

Why is there so much dishonesty in church? We pretend to be super Christians. But most of us aren't. But we all know we come up really short.

When you are in the hospital, you don't pretend to be well do you? No. You are in the hospital for surgery. You are there because you are sick.

Folks we are all sick. We are sin sick. We need a doctor. We need doctor Jesus. Doctor Jesus knows exactly where the trouble is that is keeping us from being well. He performs the procedure for healing. He does radical heart surgery and then puts us on a daily therapy program of grace and love.

Is anybody not sick? "I'm not sick." Sure you are. You are sin sick. All have sinned and come short of the glory of God. You are either a saved sinner or a condemned sinner. You are either lost in sin or saved from sin. You are on one side or the other.

You are either pre surgery and desperate in need or post surgery doing much better.

And you don't have to lie about either. A guy told me sometime ago, I'm an alcoholic—I go to AA meetings. Another guy was telling me I'm a sex addict—I go to a support group led by a counselor.

You see, it doesn't do you any good to lie. God already knows. He knows all about you and he loves you.

Just be honest and say, "God I need you. I need your grace and forgiveness. Be honest with God. He can help you when you are honest.

What is required of any real relationship? Honesty. A husband and wife can't have a marriage if there is uncertainty. Parents and children can't be real with each other without honesty. If you are dating a guy or girl, what do you want to know? You want to know the truth.

If you hire an employee, do you want someone you can trust or do you want a habitual liar? And even if a guy has some problems, if he will just say, hey…I've been a liar and a thief…but I'm really trying to get my act together, you are more likely to give that man a chance.

Jesus said in John 8:32 "And we will know the truth and the truth will set us free."

CHAPTER EIGHT
FOR REFLECTION AND MEDITATION

1. How does dishonesty enslave you?

2. How has honesty freed you?

3. Jesus liberates us. How has He given you freedom in your life?

4. What is an area in your life that you are going to be honest with before God?

5. Are you living a life of enslaving dishonesty?

6. Will you pray and ask God to help you have full truth in your life?

I Give You Perseverance

I have fought a good fight, I have finished my course, I have kept the faith, 2 Timothy 4:7. What is it that normally succeeds in making you quit? What is the one sin, the one dreaded part of life or the one emotion that topples you most every time?

What About Failure

Failure is a very deciding factor in causing us to give up. We may have tried but we didn't see any results for our efforts. We say okay, "I'm going to grow a green beautiful weed free yard this spring. We started working on it last fall and we hit it hard in the spring. We have some measure of success but the neighbor may not keep his yard pest free and weed free and they both keep coming over into our yard. And about July we may say, "Oh, what's the use."

We may not be that good in Geometry. We say, "I really need an A in Geometry." So we study hard. We do our homework and pay close attention in class but still end up with a C. Now you may feel a sense of relief that you got the C or you may feel like because you did not achieve your goal that you failed.

Sometimes we do the best we can and we still fail. We work hard, pray hard and give our best but it doesn't work out. So we say, "We tried. But it didn't happen." So therefore we quit.

Abraham Lincoln was an amazing man. He ran for local government and was defeated. He ran for state government and was defeated...several times. He ran for congress and won but then he was defeated for re-election. Finally after losing one election after another in his lifetime, Abraham Lincoln was elected as President of the United States and is remembered as one of our greatest. He had failed to achieve his goal on so many occasions. But ultimately he did not fail, because he never quit.

You haven't failed ultimately until you stop. Now that may not necessarily mean that you are a failure even when you quit. There is something about having good common sense. Here is a brick wall. You say, "I'm going to knock this brick wall down by ramming my head into it." So you run hard and hit the brick wall full force with your head. The brick wall does not budge. But your head sure hurts. You look at the wall and you think - I've failed. But, quitters never win so I'm going to hit this brick wall again and then you do it again and then you do it again. Finally your head is really hurting. And you say, "I think I've had enough. I quit. I'm a failure." No...you aren't a failure. You finally started using what was left of your head. And you said, "I stop. I quit."

There are those instances in life where it does not make sense that you keep going until you mentally and physically drop. You have to count the cost and consider if the prize is worth it.

Abraham Lincoln saw the prize as being worth it to him personally; and his leadership saved our country during very tumultuous times.

What About When You Are Tired

What makes you quit? What about when you are tired. I confess that is one of my weaknesses. I am more prone for failure when I'm exhausted...how about you? I can usually do a lot. I don't have to have eight hours sleep. But I have to have some sleep. If I'm tired then I'm more likely to put a project over to the side for a day or two.

The mind and the body both require rest. It only makes sense. Even God rested on the seventh day. We have a hard time learning and understanding we need rest. You heard about this one man that was going to take a day off and a Christian brother said, "You can't take a day off. The devil never takes a day off." And he said, "Yeah, and if I don't occasionally take a day off then I'm just like the devil."

You may have a job that requires 60 or 70 hours of work a week. You love the job but you are so tired that one day you throw in the towel.

Here is an athlete that goes every second of the game. He is a great athlete but the coach fails to bench him for a five minute break during the third quarter. Therefore when the fourth quarter comes and he really needs him, he's too tired to arise to the occasion and his legs give out and he quits on the last fast break. Not because he wants to, but because he's tired. Do you ever get tired?

What makes you tired? Work? Family? Do stresses and pressures of daily life grind you down? Are they wearing you out?

What About Discouragement

What makes you quit? What about discouragement? You heard how the devil was auctioning off his chief tools but there was one tool that he had over to the side and someone asked him, "What about that tool?" And the devil said, "That is my best tool. That is my tool of discouragement. When I have tried everything and cannot get a man, I can bring him down with that one most every time."

Too often people quit when discouraged. The devil loves it when you lose the gait in your step. He loves it when your head is hanging down and when you feel no victory in your life. He wants you to feel bad and be sad about all of your life. And sometimes it's because we have failed and we are tired or life is not going as we had hoped and we get discouraged.

Now Paul said, "I have fought the good fight. I have finished the race; I have kept the faith. Now there is in store for me the crown of righteousness, which the Lord, the righteous

Judge, will award to me on that day and not only to me, but
also to all who have longed for his appearing." 2 Timothy 4:7

Perseverance Begins With A Decision

We sing sometimes, "I have decided to follow Jesus."
The Philippian jailer that we read about in Acts 16 made a life
changing decision. Paul and Silas said, "Believe on the Lord
Jesus Christ and you will be saved." The jailer made that life
changing decision. He said, "This is what I want to do."

Do you ever make any decisions? Do you ever decide
and say, I want to buy this house or this car? Or, attend a
certain school? Or, this is the job I wish to pursue? And you
decide and go with it?

I have decided to follow Jesus. No turning back. No
turning back. Though none go with him. I still will follow.
Though none go with him I still will follow. It's a decision.

Romans 13:10 Paul would say, "Whoever calls upon
the name of the Lord will be saved." The salvation belongs to
whoever will decide for Christ.

The worst decision is no decision. Do you have trouble
making decisions? Pilate couldn't decide about Jesus. So he
says I'll just wash my hands of Jesus. Paul preached to King
Agrippa, but Agrippa couldn't decide that day. You think you
can persuade me in such a short time to be a Christian? He
asked in Acts 26:28. But he did not make a decision.

Longevity begins with a commitment. I'm going to run five
miles today. You are more apt to complete it if you make a
decision on the outset that this is what you are going to do. I'm
going to be in Church on Sunday. It's a decision. When Sunday

comes you don't have to look around and start asking, well…
it's Sunday, I wonder if there is anything to do today? No. You
already know there is something to do. You have Sunday
school and church. But it's no biggie because you made a
decision a long time ago that whenever it is at all possible that
is where you will be on the Lord's Day.

Perseverance begins with a decision. But failure is sure to
occur if there is not a clear understanding about what it is that
you want.

Perseverance continues with a decision. This is what I want
to do. *Perseverance finishes with an understanding…*this is what I
wanted to do. Perseverance begins with a commitment,
continues with a commitment and ends committed.

Commitment May Lose Its Flame

Sometimes just commitment for commitment's sake
may become drudgery.

An employee – but not a worker, he has lost his fire.

A church member – but a member not on fire.

Married – but not in love, committed to the marriage
but not in love.

On the team – but not a player.

A citizen of the country – but not patriotic.

How does perseverance make the difference? We find
new ways to make it work. We persevere in marriage. We keep
working at it. We keep recreating our marriage and discovering
new ways to love the same old person. We persevere on the
team. We find new ways to win the game. We persevere in
church. We find new ways to make the church meaningful and

interesting. We persevere in our country. We don't always like the President but we pray for and support whoever it is.

How can we persevere through the best of times and the worst of times? I say the best of times because sometimes life can be so good that you can't stand it. You have so much going for you. So much health, so much money, so much happiness that you just take it for granted and abuse it.

Knowledge – this is it. Knowing what you want. Do you know what you want? You can't persevere until you know. Paul said, "I know whom I have believed and am persuaded that he is able to keep that which I have committed unto him against that day." 2 Timothy 1:12 He said…I know.

I know what I want. I want Jesus. I know whom I am serving. I am serving Jesus. I know what my life consists of…my life consists of Jesus. I know where I am going and who will take me there – Jesus.

Awareness – Be aware of the detours, the potholes that rip you, and the distractions that beset you and knock you down. Jesus told about a man who began to build a house but he didn't count the cost. Beware of what or who discourages you and stay away from them.

Humility – Stay humble. Stay on your knees. Folks if Jesus needed to fall on his face before the Father in the garden of Gethsemane…who are we to think we don't? Jesus told about the Pharisee and the Publican. The Pharisee stood self-righteously thanking God that he was righteous, a keeper of the law and obeyed the commandments. The publican smote his breast saying, "Oh God be merciful to me a sinner." Jesus said, this is the kind of guy I can use. He went home justified before the Father. One man went home dignified before men...the other justified before God.

Adrian Rogers said, "The average American is an ego maniac strutting his way to hell thinking he is too good to be damned." In humility we have just enough insecurity to work hard to prepare but enough confidence to pull if off.

Paul realized and confessed, "I am the chief of sinners." But he also could teach, evangelize and preach anyplace without fear.

Daily – How do we endure in life? One day at a time. We cannot live tomorrow, but we can live today. You cannot change where you have been but you can make a decision about where you want to go.

We sow. Galatians 6:9 "Let us not grow tired in well doing. At the proper time we will reap a harvest if we don't quit."

The Olympic games are always a spectacle. The snow boarders going down that long pipe and the skiers and ice skaters are incredible models to us of people who stick to their stuff every day. We took Gold, Silver and bronze medals in one event in 2002. Those three young men stood on the platform and three United States flags were raised. What a moment for our country. What a moment for them. All the hours, days, weeks, years of perseverance had just resulted into Olympic medals for three men. Finally it was worth it all. They have blessed our nation and our world by their perseverance.

One of the greatest gifts you can give to a friend is to hang tough and persevere. One of the greatest gifts you can give to someone you love is to stay with it and persevere.

Some day we will stand before Jesus. We already have a mighty throng of witnesses before us the book of Hebrews tells us. And some day we will stand before Him and receive the greatest award of all when we hear Him say, "Well done, good and faithful servant. Enter into the joy of your Lord."

Today, will you willfully, openly, unashamedly love, live for, and serve Jesus Christ? You will find no greater master. There is no greater love than God's love. I invite you today to openly give your life to Him.

CHAPTER NINE
FOR REFLECTION AND MEDITATION

1. One is the one area in your life where you are about to quit?

2. Will you consider talking to someone today who might pray with you about your decision? Quitting is not always the answer.

3. Did you ever quit a relationship or another aspect of life and now regret it?

4. Who is someone who never gives up on you?

5. Perseverance is not always easy. But there are rewards. Can you think of some of the rewards of perseverance?

I Give You Peace

Mark 4:35 – 41, "That day when evening came, he said to his disciples, "Let us go over to the other side." Leaving the crowd behind, they took him along, just as he was, in the boat. There were also other boats with him. A furious quail came up, and the waves broke over the boat, so that i was nearly swamped. Jesus was in the stern, sleeping on a cushion. The disciples woke him and said to him, "Teacher don't you care if we drown?" He got up, rebuked the wind and said to the waves, "Quiet or Peace be Still! The wind died down and it was completely calm. He said to his disciples, "Why are you so afraid? Do you still have no faith?" They were terrified and asked each other, "Who is this? Even the wind and the waves obey him!"

The disciples went from fear to terror. They first feared the storm and then suddenly there was quiet and they were terrified of reality. The disciples saw a manifestation of the power of Jesus.

The peace brought about quiet and calm. In the peace they saw Jesus. God has a way of revealing himself in the quiet moments of life. You turn off the television and open the Bible. The family gathers around the table. You get quiet and there is prayer. A hush comes over the hospital room. Here is a dear saint breathing her last breaths…she is slipping slowly out into eternity. God is felt in the room. You know He is there.

In the midst of their peace the disciples began to develop a theology about Jesus. They started thinking and asking questions, "Who is this?" Such a radical command of nature made them take serious notice of this humble man in the boat. "Wait - this carpenter is not just anybody," they were saying. A theology professor asks a lot of questions and doesn't always give all the answers. That's why God gave us the Holy Spirit and prayer and His word. We go to God in prayer and search the guidance of the Holy Spirit and trust God for His understanding.

When Jesus ascended into heaven, the disciples began a study of the gospels? No. They didn't have the gospels. They began a study of the writings of Paul? No. Paul was lost and persecuting the church. They began an intense study of the Old Testament? Not really because Jesus came to give us a new covenant. The apostles had three keys to turn. First was the *example and teaching* of Jesus and what they remembered Him saying. Secondly, they now had the *Holy Spirit.* Jesus gave them the Holy Spirit. Third they had *prayer.* That's all they had. And they found the guidance of God upon their lives through the Holy Spirit and prayer and the example of Christ. This is why we like the television and the radio blasting…it entertains us and keeps us from thinking. When there was calm and peace the disciples starting developing their theology about Jesus. Who is this guy that brings about such calm? Have you asked that question lately?

Jesus said, in John 14:27, "Peace I leave with you; my peace I give you. I do not give to you as the world gives. Do not let your hearts be troubled and do not be afraid."

How much of the world is at peace? Is there peace in America? Is there peace in Afghanistan? Is there peace in the Middle East? Is there peace in the famine stricken lands of Africa? Where do you find peace in our world?

How many people are at peace? Almost everybody has some kind of a problem. How many churches are at peace? Today, sadly, so many congregations are unhappy.

I received an email from a pastor one day. He has been with a church about two years and all they have all done is fight. And they wonder why nobody in their community wants to come to their church and be saved. Who really wants to be like them? Who needs that? The unsaved man has enough headaches and tension of his own without being in a ruckus at church.

A man told me, he said, "Before I can do much for my family I have to get myself at peace." When the church is at peace we can reach others for Christ.

People are attracted to others at peace. We are drawn to others. I'd much rather talk to someone that is content and happy than somebody that is whining all the time. Churches get a reputation for being troubled and people stay away from them. But a church that is praying and loving and working together will attract others. The best gift we can give our community is to be at peace with each other.

The best gift you can give to your friends and the special person in your life is the gift of peace. Being at peace within yourself draws them to you. They want to be around you because your peace calms their troubled lives.

Where do we get this peace? Jesus gives it to us. He gives us something the world cannot give and the world cannot take away. Give your friends and loved ones peace. Help to experience peace in Christ. Extend to them peace. You help them to be calm and at peace and you'll have a friend forever.

This is one reason we are so attracted to Jesus. We just keep running back to Christ. He levels our lives and He puts us back together. We jump into the storms of life and then seek Him for refuge and help in times of trouble. When life is falling apart we grab for Him because He puts us back together and gives us some semblance of structure and peace about our lives.

This day extend peace to someone who may be hanging on through a turbulent storm.

CHAPTER TEN
FOR REFLECTION AND MEDITATION

1. At this moment what is creating disturbance in your life?

2. Jesus brought peace during the storms. Will you at this moment invite Him to bring peace to your life?

3. What disrupts peace?

4. How might you today be used to bring about peace to a person with a turbulent life or stress-filled situation?

5. How is the peace of Christ different from that of the world?

Notes

Notes

Notes

Notes

Words and Comments from Special People

Words and Comments from Special People

Words and Comments from Special People

www.ingramcontent.com/pod-product-compliance
Lightning Source LLC
Chambersburg PA
CBHW032143040426
42449CB00005B/389